Contents

A Note About These Stories

The Philippines is a large group of islands in Southeast Asia. The group is nearly 2000 kilometres long, from north to south. There are more than 7000 islands in the Philippines. The most important city – the capital – is Manila, on Luzon Island.

The first people who lived on the islands caught fish and animals for food. The weather in the Philippines is hot and wet and rice grows well there. In the rainy season (June to November), rain falls every day. In the dry season (December to May), very little rain falls. People started growing rice more than 3000 years ago. Rice is still a very important crop. It is grown in wet fields on the hills and mountains. There are walls of earth and stones around each wet field. These are called terraces.

For hundreds of years, people from many different lands came to the islands. People came from India, China, Indonesia and from Arab countries. Many of these people stayed in the islands. Some of the customs and traditions from their own countries became customs and traditions in the islands. These things became part of the culture of the Philippines. For example, the Islamic religion was brought by Arabs.

Until the sixteenth century, there were many kings and rulers in the Philippines. Each king ruled a group of villages or a small island. Then in 1521, Ferdinand Magellan and his soldiers came from Spain. Magellan was killed. But a few years later, some more Spanish soldiers came. These Spanish soldiers ruled the islands for the Spanish king – King Philip the Second. This is how the Philippines got its name. The Spanish soldiers brought the Christian religion with them. Today, most people in the Philippines are Christian.

Spain ruled the Philippines for nearly 400 years. But at the end of the nineteenth century, Spain fought a war with the United States. When the war ended, Spain gave the Philippines to the USA. Soldiers from the USA and the Philippines fought together in the Second World War (1939–1945). And in 1946 the Philippines became an independent country.

There are many legends and stories about the history of the Philippines. Some stories are very old. They are about the beginning of the world. And they are about the times when people first lived in the islands of the Philippines. Many of the stories in this book are about gods and giants and monsters. Monsters were usually very ugly and frightening. They often fought and killed animals and people. Giants were huge and they were extremely strong. They often lived alone and they had to do special work for the gods. Many of the people in the stories have very strange names. These are the old names from the times before the Spanish came.

Some of the monsters and giants and animals in these stories can do magic. They can change their bodies. Or they can make special things happen. One of the stories is about a magical bird. It is called a tabon bird.

a rice terrace

a lily

durians

pineapples

a bow and arrow

a waterfall

a kris

a carabao

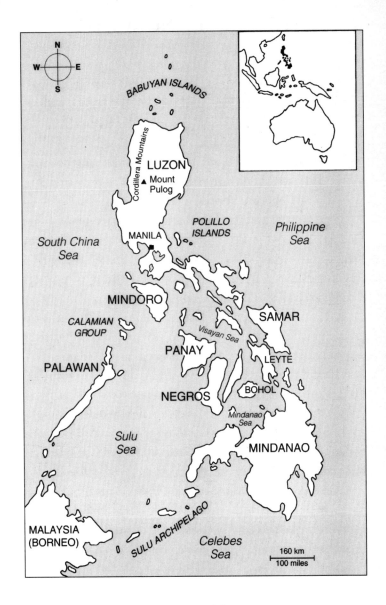

A Map of the Philippines

THE GIANT ANGNGALO

At the beginning of time, everything was dark. Heaven was above the Earth. But there was no sky between them. Heaven covered the Earth completely. Everything was silent. Everything was dark. Nothing moved.

Then, at the centre of the Earth, something began to move. Life was beginning. But what was this first life? Was it a rat? No one knows!

Time passed, and the life changed its shape many times. At last, it became the giant, Angngalo. Angngalo grew bigger and bigger. Slowly, he pushed Heaven away from the Earth. And light came between them. The giant Angngalo had made the sky!

The giant stood on the Earth. All around him was the sea. Angngalo pushed Heaven up, and up, and up! Heaven was very big and heavy. Angngalo was afraid to move. At last, he did move and Heaven crashed down. Then the sky disappeared. Everything was dark again.

So Angngalo pushed Heaven up again. After that, he could not move. He had to hold up Heaven with his arms. For many thousands of years, the giant held up Heaven. His arms became very, very tired.

One day, Angngalo moved one of his arms. And a large piece of Heaven fell into the sea! The large piece of Heaven broke into many thousands of smaller pieces.

These pieces of Heaven are the seven thousand, one hundred and seven islands which we call the Philippines.

For many thousands of years, the giant held up Heaven.

THE GIFT FROM THE GODS

A long, long time ago, a young man lived in a village in the Cordillera Mountains. His name was Kinaw-od.

Kinaw-od's father was the leader of the village. When his father died, Kinaw-od himself became the leader of his people.

The young man was strong and brave. Each day, Kinaw-od and the men of the village went up onto the high mountains. They took bows and arrows with them and they hunted for food. They killed deer, pigs and birds. All the men were good hunters. They always came back to the village with food for their families.

There was a forest near the village. Each day, the women of the village went into the forest. They picked nuts and fruits from the trees.

Time passed, and soon there were only a few animals and birds on the mountains near the village. The men had to go further and further over the mountains to hunt. And the women had to go further and further into the forests to find nuts and fruits. It was very difficult to get food.

'We must leave this village,' Kinaw-od said. 'We must find a new place to live. A place where there are no other people. A place where no hunters have been. Then we'll find food again.'

Kinaw-od and the villagers prayed to the gods.

'Help us to find a new place,' they said. 'A place where

there is food.'

Kinaw-od and his people left their village and they walked over the mountains. After many days, they came to a long valley. At the bottom of the valley, there was a river. The grass was green and there were many trees.

Kinaw-od looked across the valley. There were high mountains on the other side. Suddenly, a bird flew over his head. Quickly, Kinaw-od picked up his bow and an arrow. He pulled the string of the bow. The arrow flew into the air. The arrow hit the bird and killed it. The bird fell onto the ground by Kinaw-od's feet.

'The gods have given us a sign,' he said. 'They are telling us to stay here.'

The villagers prayed to the gods. They thanked the gods for the sign. Then they began to build houses. The villagers built houses on the side of the valley.

'We can get our water from the river,' said one of the women.

'And there's lots of wood for fires,' said another woman.

'There's fruit on the trees,' said one of the men.

'And I can hear animals in the forest,' said another man. 'This is a good place for hunting.'

Kinaw-od's people lived happily in their new village. But they went hunting every day. And soon, there were only a few animals in the forest. And there was no more fruit on the trees. Again, it was difficult to get food.

'We must move on again,' Kinaw-od said. 'We must find a new place to live.'

So they began another long journey through the mountains.

One day, they reached Mount Pulog. They began to walk through the trees and up the mountain.

'What is that wonderful smell?' asked one of the women, suddenly.

'Somebody is cooking food,' another woman replied.

The villagers followed Kinaw-od through the trees. They walked quietly and carefully. They were very hungry. And the smell of the food was very good.

They soon came to some flat ground between the trees. Strange people were cooking food on a fire. They were tall people. Their skin was whiter than the skin of Kinaw-od's people. These strangers moved quickly. When they moved, their feet did not touch the ground!

'These people must be the gods of the mountains,' whispered Kinaw-od.

Then the young man walked towards the strangers. The villagers followed him.

The tall gods smiled when they saw Kinaw-od and his people.

'Welcome,' they said. 'Please sit down and have some of our food.'

'Thank you,' said Kinaw-od. 'We are tired and very hungry.'

The gods took their cooking pots from the fire. Then they took soft white seeds from the pots and put them onto some leaves. They gave this food to the villagers.

'What strange food is this?' asked Kinaw-od.

When they moved, their feet did not touch the ground!

One of the gods smiled. 'Have you never eaten rice?' he said. 'It is a wonderful food. We grow rice. It is a kind of grass. But its seeds are good to eat.

'Please, eat some!' he went on. 'It is very good. You will like it.'

So Kinaw-od and his people ate some rice.

'It is good,' they said.

'You must grow rice,' said one of the gods. 'If you do, you won't have to move your village again. You can grow as much rice as you need. And you can keep rice for a long time. Grow rice! You will never be hungry again!'

'How do you grow this wonderful food?' asked Kinaw-od.

'First, cut down some trees,' the god told him. 'Then dig the ground. Make the ground into flat fields – terraces. After the rains come, put rice seeds in the ground. The plants will soon grow up out of the ground – green and tall. The rice will be on the tops of the plants. When the dry season comes, you can pick the rice. You can eat some of it and you can keep some of it.'

Then the gods gave the young leader a big bag. It was a bag of *palay*, or rice seed.

———

Kinaw-od and his people returned to their village in the valley. The men cut down some of the trees near the river. They built terraces – small flat fields. And they got stones from the river and built walls around the fields. When the rains came, they put the rice seeds in the ground.

At last, the dry season came. They picked the rice and

They built terraces – small flat fields.

they ate some of it. They kept the rest of the rice. They planted these rice seeds the next year. Everyone said, 'This is wonderful food.'

After that, the villagers stayed in the valley. They built more terraces near the river.

Kinaw-od got married and his wife had a son. One day, Kinaw-od's son became the leader of the village. And his people also built rice terraces.

The years passed, and more and more terraces were built.

———

Today, after three thousand years, the terraces cover many thousands of hectares. If you could put them next to each other, the terraces would be eight times as long as the Great Wall of China!

The rice terraces were built a very long time ago. But rice is still important for the people of the Philippines. It is eaten at every meal.

YUKOS AND THE MONSTER

Long, long ago, there was a monster called Mandabon. He lived in a cave on the Ampawig Mountain, near the Umayan River. All the people in the villages by the river were afraid of him.

Mandabon was a wild and terrible monster. And he was always hungry. He often stole chickens and pigs from the villagers.

The villagers were very frightened.

'Mandabon has taken all our chickens,' they said. 'Will he take our children now?'

Many of the villagers left their homes.

———

Chief Bangani lived in the biggest village. He was the leader of all the villages by the river. His people were very worried. And he was worried too.

'What can I do?' he asked himself.

Many years ago, the chief had fought the monster. But Mandabon had almost killed him. And now, Chief Bangani was not a young man.

'No! I'm not quick enough or strong enough,' he thought. 'I cannot fight Mandabon again. But there are young men in the villages by the river. Many of them are strong and quick. Is one of them brave enough? Is one of them clever enough? Can one of them kill Mandabon?'

Chief Bangani was worried about something else. He had a beautiful daughter called Buhi. He was worried about her.

'Mandabon is a problem,' thought Chief Bangani. 'And Buhi is a problem too. I have to find a good husband for her.'

One day, Chief Bangani was thinking about his problems. Suddenly, he had an idea. He knew what do!

'I'll give my daughter to the young man who kills Mandabon,' he thought. 'The young man will be brave and strong. He will marry Buhi.'

———

Soon, all the villagers had heard the news. Lots of men wanted to marry Buhi. They were all young and handsome.

'One of them will kill the monster,' thought the chief.

The first young man went up the mountain to Mandabon's cave.

'He is strong and clever,' the villagers said. 'He'll kill Mandabon.'

But they were wrong. The young man fought bravely and well, but the monster killed him.

The villagers were surprised and they were sad. The weeks passed. Many other young men went to fight Mandabon. But Mandabon was big and strong and cruel. Every one of the young men died!

'What shall I do now?' thought Chief Bangani. 'Mandabon has killed the best young men from all the villages!' The chief was very unhappy.

One evening, a young man came to Chief Bangani's house. The young man's name was Yukos.

Yukos was not very tall or very strong but he was a clever young man. He could make anything. And he could repair anything. He made fish traps for the villagers. The villagers used his traps to catch fish in the Umayan River.

Yukos stood in front of Chief Bangani.

'Sir,' he said. 'I will kill the monster, Mandabon.'

'You?' said Chief Bangani. He was surprised.

'Yes,' said Yukos. 'I cannot fight him. But I can trap him. I know about making traps. I will trap Mandabon. Then he will not be able to fight. It will be easy to kill him.'

'You are very brave, Yukos,' said Chief Bangani. 'Do you know what you are going to do? Remember, many of your friends have died. Mandabon has killed them easily.'

'Sir,' said Yukos. 'I've thought for a long time. I have a plan, I will succeed!'

'All right, Yukos,' said Chief Bangani. 'Go and try to kill the monster. I will pray to the gods. I will ask them to help you.'

At that moment, Buhi came into the room. She smiled at Yukos. She knew about the young man. She had heard good things about him.

Buhi was carrying a piece of beautiful cloth in her hands. 'Please take this cloth,' she said. 'Wear it on your head. It is a very special. When you wear it, nothing can hurt you.'

'Thank you,' said Yukos. 'I will wear it.' He took the special cloth and tied it round his head.

'I will kill Mandabon!' he thought. 'I know it. And I

Yukos took the special cloth and tied it round his head.

will marry Buhi!'

Yukos left Chief Bagani's house immediately.

———

Early next morning, Yukos started to walk to the Ampawig Mountain. He took with him a very long piece of thin rope.

Soon, he met an old woman. She was standing beside the Umayan River.

'Will you carry me across the river?' she asked.

'Yes, I will,' replied Yukos.

Carefully, he picked up the old woman and he carried her across the river.

'I know where you are going, Yukos,' the old woman said. 'And I know what you are going to do. The monster, Mandabon, is very dangerous. But I'm going to give you a magic *kris*. You will kill the monster easily with this special knife.'

'Thank you,' said Yukos. Then he took the big knife. And he said goodbye to the old woman.

Now the young man had a magic kris and the special cloth. He walked on up the Ampawig Mountain.

'Now I will kill Mandabon!' he thought bravely.

At last, Yukos reached the monster's cave.

Mandabon was asleep. But he was making a loud noise. He was snoring!

Yukos was afraid. But he moved quickly and quietly. He took the thin rope and tied it across the front of the cave. First he tied it on the right side. Then he tied it on the left side. He went backwards and forwards with the rope. He

21

was making a huge net across the front of the cave. It was a very big fish trap!

At last the net was finished.

'Mandabon!' shouted Yukos. 'Come out and fight, you cruel monster!'

Mandabon opened his eyes. He did not like people who woke him up. He was very angry. He gave a terrible shout.

Then the monster jumped up and ran to the front of the cave. And he ran straight into the net! His head was caught in the rope. His arms were caught in the rope. And his feet were caught too! He pulled and pulled, but he could not get out of the net. Mandabon was trapped!

Quickly, Yukos took the magic kris and cut off Mandabon's head.

————

Later that day, the villagers saw Yukos. He was carrying Mandabon's head. He held it high in the air. Everyone saw the head. And they were very happy.

The young man went to Chief Bangani's village. All the villagers welcomed him.

'Yukos has killed the monster!' they said. 'Now we can live in peace!'

And the people shouted and sang songs. They danced and they played music.

Chief Bangani heard the noise and he came out of his house. 'What is happening?' he asked.

'Yukos has killed the monster!' the villagers shouted. 'Mandabon is dead!'

Mandabon was trapped!

Chief Bangani saw the monster's head. He spoke to Yukos kindly.

'You are a brave young man, Yukos,' he said. 'You will marry my daughter, Buhi.'

So Buhi and Yukos got married. Their wedding celebrations went on for many days. The two young people were very happy. And the villagers were happy too. Everyone liked Yukos.

'Buhi has a brave and clever husband,' everyone said.

And when Bagani died a few years later, Yukos became the new chief.

BAROM-MAI

There was once a man called Barom-mai. He was a king in the Visayan Islands. Barom-mai was a good king, but he was very ugly.

Barom-mai was not married.

'My daughter cannot marry a man as ugly as you!' said one father to King Barom-mai. And many of the fathers of beautiful young women said the same thing.

But there was one man who did not say that. His name was Tageb. He was also a king in the Visayan Islands. He was not very handsome himself. But he did have a very beautiful daughter! Her name was Madayaw-bayho.

'Barom-mai is a good man,' King Tageb said. 'My daughter will marry him. He will be kind to Madayaw-bayho. Kindness is more important than a handsome face!'

Madayaw-bayho did not like King Barom-mai's ugly face. But she loved her father, and she wanted to please him.

'I will marry Barom-mai,' she said.

So King Barom-mai and Madayaw-bayho got married. Barom-mai loved his beautiful young wife. He was always kind to her. He gave her many gifts.

Madayaw-bayho wanted to love her husband, but she could not. She was polite and helpful. But she was very sad. She could not look at her husband's ugly face.

One day, King Barom-mai spoke to his wife.

'Why are you so sad?' he asked.

'Husband, I want to see my friends and my family,' replied Madayaw-bayho.

The king wanted to make his wife happy.

'Go and visit your family for a few days,' he said.

So Madayaw-bayho went to her father's palace. She was happy to see her family again. And she would not go back to Barom-mai.

King Tageb did not know what to do. He sent messages to King Barom-mai.

First, he wrote, 'Madayaw-bayho is busy.'

Another day, he wrote, 'My daughter is sick.'

A few weeks later, he wrote, 'Madayaw-bayho must go to her friend's wedding celebration.'

But King Barom-mai knew the truth and he was very unhappy. He loved Madayaw-bayho. He wanted her to come back.

'How can I make my wife love me?' Barom-mai asked himself.

The people who advised the king could not help him.

'You were very kind to the queen, sir,' said one of these advisers.

'You gave the queen the best rooms in the palace,' said another adviser.

'You gave the queen many expensive gifts and fine clothes,' said the third adviser.

King Barom-mai sent the advisers away. He called for a shaman. The shaman was a clever man. He helped people with their problems. He made sick people better.

'I am ugly,' said the king. 'My wife cannot love me.

Can you change my face? Can you make me handsome?'

The shaman did not laugh at the king. He did not smile.

'I cannot help you, sir,' he said. 'But there is someone who can help you. There is an old man who lives in a cave on Apo Mountain. He does magic things. He can make the queen love you.'

'I must speak to this old man!' said the king.

———

The next day, Barom-mai began his journey to Apo Mountain. He took some men with him. They travelled through dark forests. At last, they climbed up the mountain. On the side of the mountain they found a cave. It was the cave where the old man lived.

The old man was thin. He had small black eyes and a long white beard. Barom-mai told the old man about his problem.

'I am ugly,' he said. 'The queen cannot love me because I am ugly. Can you make her love me?'

The old man thought for a few moments.

'There is a way to make her love you,' he replied. 'But it will not be easy.'

'What must I do?' asked the king. 'I'll do anything!'

'You must bring me three things,' the old man said. 'Bring me the egg of a black *tabon* bird. Bring me the milk of a white *carabao* – a white water buffalo. And bring me a flower from the Tree of Imagination.'

'How will these things help me?' said King Barom-mai. 'Will they give me the queen's love?'

'The egg of the tabon bird will make the queen gentle,' said the old man. 'The milk of the white carabao will make her kind. And the flower of the Tree of Imagination will make her love your face.'

'Where can I find all these things?' asked the king.

'The black tabon bird lives at the top of this mountain,' replied the old man. 'You must find its nest. At the bottom of the mountain lives an old woman. Try to find her. She has a white carabao.'

'And the Tree of Imagination? Where is that?' asked Barom-mai.

'I cannot tell you where that is,' said the old man. 'It will be very difficult to find. Only painters, musicians and writers have seen it.'

King Barom-mai was unhappy. He was not a painter, or a writer, or a musician.

'But I love Madayaw-bayho,' he said. 'And I want her to come back. I will try to find these things!'

The king and his men climbed to the top of the mountain. They saw a huge black bird sitting on a nest. The huge nest was made of the leaves and branches of a tree.

For two days, Barom-mai and his men watched the bird. They waited and waited. But the tabon bird did not move. Then, on the third day, they saw another huge black bird. It was flying high in the sky. The bird on the nest made a loud cry. Then it flew up into the sky. Both the tabon birds flew away.

King Barom-mai moved quickly and quietly. He went to the nest and he looked inside it. There was an egg in

They saw a huge black bird sitting on a nest.

the nest – a very large egg. It was the colour of gold. Carefully, the king took the egg from the nest. Then he and his men climbed down the mountain.

When they arrived at the bottom of the mountain, the king and his men looked for the old woman and her white carabao. At last, they found the animal. It was outside a temple. The king went into the temple and he found the old woman.

'I need some milk from your carabao,' he told her.

'I will give you some milk,' replied the old woman. 'If you want to do something good, the milk will help you.'

The king thanked the woman. He left the temple and he took some milk from the white carabao.

'Now, the most difficult thing,' Barom-mai said. 'How am I going to find the Tree of Imagination? How will I see it? I'm not a painter, or a musician, or a writer.'

The king and his men left Apo Mountain, and they travelled towards the coast.

———

That evening, King Barom-mai sat down by the sea. He thought about Madayaw-bayho. He thought about her unhappy face and her sad eyes.

'I want her to be happy!' he said to himself. 'I want her to laugh. I want her to sing.'

Barom-mai began to imagine Queen Madayaw-bayho. He could see her! She was a picture in his head! There were flowers in her hair. She was happy and smiling. Then she began to sing, and her words were beautiful.

'How lovely she is,' thought Barom-mai.

'How lovely she is,' thought Barom-mai.

The picture in the king's head was very clear. He wanted to take a flower from Madayaw-bayho's hair. He moved forward and held out his hand. Yes! He could pick a flower out of her hair! He did it! And at that moment, the music stopped. The picture in Barom-mai's head disappeared.

The king was very sad. Then he looked down at his hand. He was holding a beautiful flower. A real flower! It had a sweet smell.

Barom-mai knew what it was.

'This is the flower from the Tree of Imagination,' he said.

The next morning, the king began his journey back to Apo Mountain. He was going to the old man's cave. He carried three things with him. The egg from the black tabon bird. The milk from the white carabao. And the flower from the Tree of Imagination.

The king and his men climbed up to the cave.

'You have come back,' said the old man.

'I have brought you the egg and the milk and the flower,' said King Barom-mai.

The old man took the egg. Carefully, he made a hole in one end. Then he put the carabao's milk into the hole in the egg. Finally, he put the flower in too. Then he gave the egg back to the king.

'Take the egg into the garden of your palace,' the old man said. 'Put it in the ground. The egg will grow into a tree. Soon, some wonderful fruits will grow on the tree. Take one of the fruits to King Tageb's palace. Give it to your wife. Ask her to eat it. It will make her love you.

Then she will go back home with you.'

'Thank you, old man,' said the king. 'How can I pay you? What can I give you?'

The old man smiled. 'When your wife returns to your palace, you must have a celebration,' he said. 'You must ask me to come to the celebration.'

'Yes, I will!' said the King Barom-mai. 'I'll be happy to see you.'

———

The king returned to his palace. He took the egg into his garden and he put it in the ground. After one day, a tree began to grow. The next morning, the king went to look at his tree. There was a wonderful smell coming from it. And on the tree there were many beautiful golden fruits. Each fruit was as big as a tabon's egg. One fruit fell onto the ground. It broke open.

King Barom-mai picked up a piece of the fruit. Inside, the fruit was the colour of milk. The king ate the piece of fruit. It was sweet. And suddenly, Barom-mai was very happy.

He wanted to give some of the fruit to Queen Madayaw-bayho immediately. Quickly, he went to King Tageb's palace. He gave one of the fruits to his wife.

Queen Madayaw-bayho ate the fruit. And suddenly, she loved her husband!

'He is a very handsome man!' she thought.

Happily, she returned to her husband's palace. The days passed. And the king and queen were very happy together.

One day, King Barom-mai called his servants. He told

On the tree there were many beautiful golden fruits.

them to cook lots of food.

'We will have a celebration,' he said. 'The queen has come home!'

But Barom-mai forgot to ask the old man to come to his celebration.

The old man was angry.

'The king has forgotten me,' he said to himself. 'I will punish him. I'll give the fruit sharp thorns. When anyone opens the fruit, the thorns will hurt their hands. And I'll give the fruit a terrible smell. No one will want to eat it!'

Today, this fruit still grows. We call it the *durian*. Durians have a sweet taste. But their skins are hard and they have sharp thorns. And durians have a terrible smell!

PINANG

Long, long ago there was a woman called Aling Rosa. Her husband was dead – she was a widow. Aling Rosa had a young daughter called Pinang. She loved her daughter very much.

Aling Rosa worked hard, and she took care of Pinang very well. She cooked the food. She washed the clothes. She cleaned the house. But Pinang never helped her mother with the housework.

When Pinang was twelve, Aling Rosa thought about her daughter's life.

'Pinang will soon be a young woman,' she thought. 'She must learn about housework now.'

So Aling Rosa tried to teach Pinang to cook. And she tried to teach her daughter to wash clothes. But Pinang was not interested in housework. Pinang wanted to play outside in the sun. She wanted to play with her friends.

'Pinang, you must watch me and learn,' Aling Rosa told her daughter. 'You will soon be a young woman. You must learn about housework.'

Pinang watched her mother for a few minutes. Then she said, 'That's easy, Mother! I can do that.'

And she ran outside to play with her friends.

Each day, Aling Rosa asked Pinang to help her to clean the floor. She asked Pinang to clean the cooking pots. Pinang did these things, but she did them badly. Aling Rosa had to clean the floor and the pots again.

'That's easy, Mother! I can do that.'

One day, Aling Rosa was ill. She could not get out of her bed. Pinang brought her mother some fresh water. Then she went to see her friends. But she did not play with her friends for very long. She went home early.

'Will you cook some rice, Pinang?' asked Aling Rosa.

'All right,' said Pinang.

The young girl took some rice and put it in the cooking pot. Then she put some water in the pot. She put the pot on the fire. But after a few minutes, Pinang heard her friends playing outside. She went out to see them. She forgot about the rice.

When the rice was cooked, no one took the pot off the fire. Pinang was with her friends. Aling Rosa was asleep. Soon, the rice was burnt. Later, Aling Rosa tried to eat it, but it was not good.

'Pinang has never cooked rice before,' Aling Rosa said to herself. 'Next time, it will be better.'

Aling Rosa was ill for many days. Pinang did more and more work in the house. She cooked all the meals. She cleaned the floor and she washed the clothes. She did not do these things very well, but Aling Rosa was pleased with her.

Pinang loved her mother. But she hated the housework. She did the housework very quickly. She did not do it well. Often, she lost things.

One day, Pinang lost the large wooden cooking spoon.

She looked for it everywhere. But she did not look carefully. She could not find the spoon.

'I can't cook the rice this evening,' she said to her mother. 'I can't find the cooking spoon.'

Aling Rosa was very ill that day. She became angry.

'Do you have eyes?' she shouted. 'Look for the spoon! Use your eyes! Or get some new ones! Then you will be able to find things!'

Pinang was angry too. She ran out of the house.

Soon it was dark, but Pinang did not return home. Aling Rosa got out of her bed and went to the door. She could hear her daughter's friends. They were playing by the river.

'Pinang must be by the river too,' Aling Rosa thought. 'She'll come home soon.'

She ate some cold rice. Then she went back to bed.

Pinang did not return that night. And she did not return the next morning. Aling Rosa was very worried. She called to her neighbour.

'Have you seen Pinang?' she asked.

'No,' replied her neighbour. 'I haven't seen her.'

Nobody knew where Pinang was. The people of the village looked for her by the river. They looked for her in the forest. They could not find Pinang anywhere.

Aling Rosa's neighbour came to take care of the widow. When she was well again, Aling Rosa also went to look for Pinang. But she did not find her.

'Is she dead?' Aling Rosa asked herself. 'Has she died in the river? Has an animal eaten her? Oh, why was I angry with her?'

Aling Rosa loved her daughter, Pinang, very much.

And now she was very unhappy.

One day, Aling Rosa saw a strange plant growing near the house.

'I've never seen that plant before,' she said to her neighbour.

'It's strange!' said her neighbour. 'Where did it come from?'

'I don't know,' said Aling Rosa.

But she took care of the plant. She gave it water every day. Soon there was a small fruit on it. Then the fruit began to grow bigger.

'It's a strange fruit!' thought Aling Rosa. 'It has the shape of a girl's head! And it is covered with eyes!'

The fruit had a yellow skin. There were brown marks on the skin.

One day, Aling Rosa and her neighbour were looking at the fruit.

'The fruit makes me think of – of Pinang!' said Aling Rosa.

Now she remembered her last words to Pinang. 'Use your eyes!' she had said. 'Or get some new ones!'

'Is Pinang now a fruit with many eyes?' said Aling Rosa. 'Did my words make this happen? Oh, no!'

She began to cry. Her tears fell on the plant. She looked at its leaves. They made her think of Pinang's arms!

Aling Rosa never saw her daughter again. But she looked after the plant very carefully. When she looked at the plant, she thought about her daughter. So she called

'Is Pinang now a fruit with many eyes?'

the fruit Pinang.

Later, more fruit grew on the plant. Aling Rosa ate some of the fruit. It was very sweet.

Aling Rosa's neighbours cut small pieces from the plant. They put them in the ground. Soon they had their own plants. They also called the fruit Pinang.

The years passed. People forgot Aling Rosa and her daughter. But the fruit of the plant was still called *pinang*. Later, the name pinang became *pinya*. This word is still used in the Philippines today. In English, the fruit is called pineapple.

SAM-IT AND THE LILY ROPE

Many years ago, there was a young woman called Sam-it. She lived in a little house near the Bued River canyon. The canyon was a very, very deep valley. The Bued River was at the bottom of the canyon.

Sam-it lived with her stepmother. Her own mother had died when Sam-it was twelve. Her father had married a second wife. This woman became Sam-it's stepmother. Now, Sam-it's father was dead too.

Sam-it lived with her stepmother, but she did not have a happy life. Every day, Sam-it cooked the meals and cleaned the house. She got all the wood for the fires. She got all the water. The water came from a spring very close to the edge of the canyon. Sam-it worked hard every day. There was a lot for her to do. In the evenings, she was very tired.

Sam-it's stepmother was an evil woman. Sam-it was afraid of her stepmother. Everyone was afraid of Sam-it's stepmother. She talked to the *ampasit* – the evil spirits who brought sickness and trouble to people. No one ever came to Sam-it's house.

Every morning, Sam-it went to the spring to fill her water jar. She liked going to the spring. It was very peaceful there. There were rocks and green trees round the spring. And beautiful white lily flowers grew near the water.

One morning, Sam-it's stepmother smiled at her. 'Pick

some lily flowers when you go to the spring,' she said. 'Tie the lilies together – make a garland. I will give the garland to the ampasit.'

That morning, a young man stopped to drink at the spring. He saw Sam-it picking the white lilies.

'This girl is very beautiful,' he thought.

Sam-it saw the young man looking at her. But she could not speak to him. He was a stranger. She did not speak to strangers.

But she could not forget the young man. For the first time, Sam-it's eyes were bright and happy. She sang songs as she walked home. Sam-it was in love!

She was still singing when she got home.

'Why are singing, child?' Sam-it's stepmother asked angrily. 'Why are you so happy?'

'Oh, the trees by the spring were so fresh and green today,' Sam-it replied. 'The lilies were white and they had a sweet smell.' And she gave her stepmother a beautiful garland of lilies and leaves.

The next morning, the young man came to the spring again. He smiled and spoke to Sam-it.

'My name is Tinong,' he said.'

Sam-it did not speak, but she smiled at him.

After that, Tinong came to the spring every morning. Sam-it and Tinong talked together every day.

One day, Tinong held Sam-it's hands. He looked into her eyes.

'I love you very much, Sam-it,' he said. 'Will you be my wife?'

'My name is Tinong,' he said.

'Oh, Tinong, I cannot be your wife,' she replied. 'My stepmother will not let me marry you. I have to look after her. I have to do all the housework.'

'I'll build a house for us,' said Tinong. 'The house will be close to your stepmother's house. Then you will be able —'

'No! She won't let me marry you,' said Sam-it, sadly. 'She'll never let me go.'

'Please, ask her if I can marry you, Sam-it,' said Tinong.

Sam-it put her hands over her eyes.

'I'm afraid of my stepmother,' she said. 'She is an evil woman. She speaks to the ampasit.'

Tinong held Sam-it's hands again.

'Let's run away!' he said. 'We will go far away! Then she will not be able to hurt you.'

'We cannot run away,' cried Sam-it. 'My stepmother will find us! The ampasit will speak to her. They will tell her where we are.'

Tinong looked at the deep canyon.

'If we climb down into the canyon, the river will quickly take us away from here. But how can we climb down to the river?' asked Tinong.

'I can make a rope!' said Sam-it. 'I can make one in a day or two.'

'I'll get a boat and I'll leave it on the river,' said Tinong. 'Then I'll come for you, Sam-it. We will climb down to the boat. We will travel at night. Your stepmother will not see us. Will you come with me, Sam-it?'

'Oh, yes!' said Sam-it. 'I will come.'

'Three nights from today, we will go,' said Tinong.

———

The next afternoon, Sam-it went to the forest. She collected lots of vines. She started to make these long, strong plants into a rope.

'I will put lilies into the rope,' she thought. 'If my stepmother comes, I will say, "I am making a garland for the ampasit.". She will not know why I am making the rope.'

Her stepmother did not come. But when Sam-it returned home that evening, her stepmother was angry.

'Why were you away so long, Sam-it?' she asked.

'I'm making a special garland for the ampasit,' Sam-it replied.

The next afternoon, Sam-it went to the forest again. She collected more vines and picked some more lilies.

On the morning of the third day, Sam-it finished the rope. Tinong helped her to carry it to the edge of the canyon. He tied one end of the rope to a tree next to the spring.

'When it is dark, I'll wait on the path near your house,' Tinong told Sam-it. 'I will make the sound of a bird. Come when you hear the cry of a bird!'

Sam-it smiled. 'I will come,' she said. 'And then we will be together forever!'

———

That night, Sam-it put her clothes and some other things into a box. Then she sat down and she waited.

Suddenly, she heard the cry of a bird.

'Tinong has come!' she thought. 'He's calling me!'

47

She ran out of the door. She ran along the path towards the canyon. It was a beautiful night and the moon was shining brightly.

Tinong was waiting by the path. Together, the young people ran to the spring. The lilies were white in the moonlight.

'How beautiful the world is tonight,' said Tinong.

Sam-it and Tinong went to the edge of the canyon. They began to climb down the rope of green vines and beautiful white flowers. Carefully, they climbed down towards the river.

'Soon we will be in the boat,' said Tinong.

Suddenly, they heard a scream!

Sam-it and Tinong looked up.

'It's my stepmother!' cried Sam-it.

Sam-it's evil stepmother was standing at the edge of the canyon. She had seen them!

Quickly, the two young people jumped down into the boat. At that moment, water came crashing down from above! Sam-it's stepmother had asked the ampasit to help her. The ampasit had broken the rocks round the spring. Now the water from the spring was falling into the canyon. It was falling over the rope.

But the river quickly carried the boat and Tinong and Sam-it away. After a minute, the young people looked back. They looked at the top of the canyon.

'Tinong! Look!' cried Sam-it. 'The lily rope has gone!'

Where the rope had been, there was a beautiful white waterfall. Sam-it's stepmother had disappeared!

'It's my stepmother!' cried Sam-it.

No one ever saw Sam-it's stepmother again. Sam-it and Tinong got married. They lived happily together for many years.

The Bued River people looked at the white waterfall. And they looked up at the white lilies which grew at the top of it. They remembered Sam-it's wedding celebration – her bridal day. And the Bued River people remembered the white flowers in Sam-it's hand. They remembered her white dress and the white veil over her face. And they called the waterfall, the Bridal Veil Falls.

The waterfall is still there today.

CLEVER ASIN

King Bato of Bukidnon had a large palace. There were beautiful grounds all around it. In the grounds, there were many gardens and lakes.

The king had many servants. Some servants picked up the leaves in the palace grounds. Some servants cooked big meals for celebrations at the palace. And some servants cleaned the floors and stairs and rooms in the palace. Everyone was busy!

A young man called Asin was one of King Bato's servants. He was a very clever young man. He was clever and quick. He often found the answer to a problem before anyone else. Yes, Asin was clever. But he wanted everyone to know about it.

'Give me something important to do,' he said to the other servants. 'I am very clever. I want to do important work.'

'Be quiet, Asin,' the other servants told him. 'You haven't been the king's servant for very long. You can't do important work.' And they gave him easy, boring things to do.

'I will make them understand,' Asin said to himself. 'I will show them how clever I am!'

Asin went to the palace kitchens. He spoke to the servants who were cooking the food.

'How many people are coming for the meal tonight?' he asked them.

They told him.

'You will need one hundred and twenty plates, twenty chickens and four pigs,' said Asin. 'And rice. You will need—'

'We know how to cook a meal,' the cooks said. 'We've done it before. Go away, Asin!'

So Asin went to see some other servants. They were making mats for the floors of the palace. Asin started to tell them how to make mats.

'Be quiet, Asin!' the servants said. 'We know how to make mats. We've been making mats for years. Go away!'

———

One day, King Bato heard about Asin. All the servants were talking about him.

'I'll give him something very difficult to do!' thought the king. 'I'll stop him making all the other servants angry.'

The king called Asin, and the young man went to see him immediately.

'I will show the king how clever I am!' thought Asin.

'We will see how clever he is!' thought the king.

King Bato looked at Asin and asked, 'Are you clever, Asin?'

'Yes, sir,' said Asin. 'I am very clever.'

The king smiled.

'Then I have a problem for you,' he said.

The king called another servant and he pointed to Asin.

'Give this young man a chicken,' he said.

Quickly, the servant brought a chicken and he gave it

to Asin. The chicken was making a loud noise.

'Kill this chicken, Asin,' said the king. 'Then make fifty meals with it. Fifty *different* meals!'

Asin held the noisy bird and he looked at it.

'I've never killed anything before,' he thought. But he did not tell the king about that. He took a small metal nail from his pocket.

'Sir, this is an easy problem,' he said. 'But first, you must make a cooking pot and a knife from this nail.'

The king looked at the nail. He did not know what to do.

'I'm busy now. Come and see me again tomorrow, Asin,' he said.

The next day, Asin went back to the palace.

'I am going to give you a different problem today,' said King Bato. 'I want you to catch the waves of the sea in a net. Bring the waves to me here.'

Asin thought for a moment. Then he replied, 'Sir, this is an easy problem. But first, you must give me a net made of sand.'

The king was angry.

'This young man is laughing at me!' he thought.

He stood up and he shouted at the young man.

'Go away, Asin!' he shouted. 'Leave the palace immediately. Don't come back! If the guards see you standing on any of my ground again, you will go to prison. Do you hear me, Asin?'

'Yes, sir,' said Asin.

But the next day, the king looked out of a window. He

saw Asin outside the palace.

The king was very angry. He ran out of the palace and he called his guards. They all went up to Asin. The young man was standing on some fresh earth.

'I told you not to come to here again!' the king shouted. 'You are standing on my ground again! You will go to prison!'

'Please, sir, I'm not standing on your ground,' replied Asin. 'I'm standing on my *own* ground.'

The young man pointed to his feet.

'This earth comes from my own garden,' he said. 'I dug it this morning.'

Suddenly, King Bato laughed.

'Come to the palace tomorrow,' he said. 'I will give you another problem.'

———

Early the next morning, Asin went to the palace. He went to the king's room. He was surprised. There was a large melon on the floor. Near it, there was a large jar with a small neck at the top.

'I want you to put the melon into the jar,' said the king. 'You must not break the jar and you must not break the melon.'

It was a large jar, but the neck at the top of the jar was very narrow. It was too narrow. Asin could not push the melon into the jar.

'This is an easy problem, sir,' said Asin. 'But I must have a few weeks to do it. Then I will bring the jar with the melon inside it.'

'I'm standing on my own ground.'

'Goodbye, Asin,' said the king. And he smiled.

'He won't come back!' the king thought.

Asin went home with the melon and the jar. He sat down by his house. He sat down to think.

'How can I do this?' he thought. 'There must be an answer. There is always an answer.'

Asin looked at his garden. It was a good garden. Many fruits and vegetables were growing in the garden. There were melons growing there. Melons! Yes! The young man had an idea!

Asin quickly found a small, young melon. It was growing on a big melon plant. The melon was the size of a bird's egg. Very carefully, Asin put the melon through the neck of the jar. He did not break the fruit from the plant.

After that, Asin gave the melon plant some water every day. The fruit grew quickly. After a few weeks, it filled the whole jar. The fruit was large and round. The melon was in the jar. And the jar was not broken!

Asin cut the melon from the plant. Then he took the jar to the king.

King Bato was surprised. 'How did you do this?' he asked Asin.

Asin told him, and the king smiled.

'So it is a different melon!' he said. 'But you are a clever young man, Asin. It was a very difficult problem and you found the answer!'

'There is always an answer, sir,' said Asin.

———

After that, Asin became the king's adviser. He helped

The melon was in the jar. And the jar was not broken!

King Bato with many difficult problems. There was always an answer! Soon, Asin was an important man.

'At last, I have important things to do,' he said.

Points for Understanding

THE GIANT ANGNGALO

1 What happened when Angngalo pushed Heaven up from the Earth?
2 One day, the giant's arms became very tired. What happened next?

THE GIFT FROM THE GODS

1 Who was Kinaw-od? Where did he live?
2 What did the men do each day?
3 What did the women do each day?
4 Why did Kinaw-od and his people have to leave the village?
5 'The gods have given us a sign,' said Kinaw-od. What was the sign?
6 What did the villagers do?
7 Kinaw-od and his people reached Mount Pulog.
   (a) What did they smell?
   (b) Who did they see?
8 What was *palay*?
9 How did Kinaw-od get palay?
10 What did Kinaw-od's people have to do with the palay?
11 What are eight times as long as the Great Wall of China?

YUKOS AND THE MONSTER

1 Who was Mandabon?
2 Where did he live?
3 What did he do?

4 Why did Chief Bangani not fight Mandabon?
5 Chief Bangani had an idea. What was his idea?
6 Describe Yukos.
7 What did Yukos take to the Ampawig Mountain?
8 How did Yukos kill Mandabon?
9 What did the villagers do when Yukos returned from the Ampawig Mountain?
10 What did Chief Bangani say to Yukos?

BAROM-MAI

1 What was Barom-mai's problem?
2 Who was Madayaw-bayho?
3 Why did Madayaw-bayho leave her husband?
4 King Tageb sent three messages to Barom-mai. What did he say in these messages?
5 Who told Barom-mai to go to Apo Mountain?
6 Who was on Apo Mountain?
7 What did Barom-mai have to do?
8 Barom-mai got two things. What were they? How did he get them?
9 What was the third thing? Why was this difficult to get?
10 What happened when Barom-mai returned to his palace?
11 What did Barom-mai give to Madayaw-bayho? What happened then?
12 What did Barom-mai forget?
13 What is good about durians? What is bad about them?

PINANG

1 Describe Pinang and her family.
2 What did Aling Rosa try to teach Pinang?
3 How did Pinang do her work?

4 Why could Pinang not cook the rice when Aling Rosa was ill?
5 What did Aling Rosa say to her daughter?
6 What started to grow near the house?
7 What shape and colour did this thing have?
8 What did Aling Rosa say about it?
9 What did Aling Rosa do?
10 What does *pinya* mean?

SAM-IT AND THE LILY ROPE

1 Where did Sam-it live?
2 Who did she live with?
3 What did Sam-it do every day?
4 What/Who were the *ampasit*?
5 Who talked to the ampasit?
6 What was at the spring?
7 Why did Sam-it have to make a garland?
8 What was it made of?
9 Who was Tinong?
10 What did he ask Sam-it?
11 What was Tinong's plan?
12 'If my stepmother comes, I will say, "I am making a garland for the ampasit.", ' said Sam-it. This was not true. What did Sam-it make and why did she make it?
13 The two young people jumped down into the boat. What happened next?
14 How did the Bued River people remember Sam-it and Tinong?

CLEVER ASIN

1 Where did Asin work?
2 'I am very clever,' said Asin. What did he want to do?
3 What did Asin say to
   (a) the cooks in the kitchens?
   (b) the servants who were making mats?
4 The king called Asin.
   (a) What did Asin think?
   (b) What did the king think?
5 What was Asin's first problem? What was his answer?
6 What was Asin's second problem? What was his answer?
7 The king was angry. What did he tell Asin?
8 What happened the next day?
9 What did Asin tell the king?
10 How did Asin get the melon into the jar with the narrow neck?

ELEMENTARY LEVEL

A Christmas Carol *by Charles Dickens*
Riders of the Purple Sage *by Zane Grey*
The Canterville Ghost and Other Stories *by Oscar Wilde*
Lady Portia's Revenge and Other Stories *by David Evans*
The Picture of Dorian Gray *by Oscar Wilde*
Treasure Island *by Robert Louis Stevenson*
Road to Nowhere *by John Milne*
The Black Cat *by John Milne*
The Red Pony *by John Steinbeck*
The Stranger *by Norman Whitney*
Tales of Horror *by Bram Stoker*
Frankenstein *by Mary Shelley*
Silver Blaze and Other Stories *by Sir Arthur Conan Doyle*
Tales of Ten Worlds *by Arthur C. Clarke*
The Boy Who Was Afraid *by Armstrong Sperry*
Room 13 and Other Ghost Stories *by M.R. James*
The Narrow Path *by Francis Selormey*
The Lord of Obama's Messenger and Other Stories
by Marguerite Siek
Why Ducks Sleep on One Leg and Other Stories *by Anne Ingram*
The Gift From the Gods and Other Stories *by Anne Ingram*
The Land of Morning Calm and Other Stories *by Anne Ingram*
Love Conquers Death and Other Stories *by Catherine Khoo and Marguerite Siek*
The Stone Lion and Other Stories *by Claire Breckon*
The Bride of Prince Mudan and Other Stories *by Celine C. Hu*

For further information on the full selection of Readers at all five levels in the series, please refer to the Heinemann ELT Guided Readers catalogue.

Macmillan Heinemann English Language Teaching, Oxford

A division of Macmillan Publishers Limited

Companies and representatives throughout the world

ISBN 0 435 27322 1

Heinemann is a registered trademark of Reed Educational & Professional Publishing Limited

The stories *The Giant Angngalo, Gift From the Gods,*
Yukos and the Monster, Barom-mai and the Durian, Pinang,
Sam-it and the Lily Rope and *Clever Asin* were first published
by Heinemann Southeast Asia
(a member of the Reed Elsevier plc group)
in **The Golden Legends of the Philippines** by Anne Ingram (1996)
© Anne Ingram 1996

These retold versions by John Escott for Heinemann ELT Guided Readers
Text © Reed Educational and Professional Publishing Limited 1997
Design and illustration
© Reed Educational and Professional Publishing Limited 1997
First published 1997

Illustrated by Michael Charlton
Illustrations and map, pages 6 and 7, by John Gilkes
Typography by Sue Vaudin
Cover by Andrew Holmes and Marketplace Design
Typeset in 11.5/14.5pt Goudy
Printed and bound in Spain by Mateu Cromo

99 00 01 02 10 9 8 7 6 5 4 3